Injured Workers' Guide

TO MINNESOTA WORKERS' COMPENSATION

Minnesota's Voice for the Injured

Copyright © 2023 Publishing.
All Rights Reserved.

No part of this publication may be reproduced, distributed, or transmitted in any form or by any means, including photocopying, recording, or other electronic or mechanical methods, or by any information storage and retrieval system without the prior written permission of the publisher, except in the case of very brief quotations embodied in critical reviews and certain other noncommercial uses permitted by copyright law.

ISBN: 978-0-578-23119-8

Schedule a Meeting
1.855.354.2667
763.421.8226
admin@mottazlaw.com

Our Office Practices in these Areas:

- Workers' Compensation
- Social Security Disability
- Employment Law

Best Lawyers
LAWYER OF THE YEAR
DAVID B. KEMPSTON
WORKERS' COMPENSATION LAW - CLAIMANTS
MINNEAPOLIS
2023

Best Lawyers
BEST LAW FIRMS
U.S.News & WORLD REPORT
WORKERS' COMPENSATION LAW - CLAIMANTS - TIER 1
MINNEAPOLIS
2023

Best Lawyers
LAWYER OF THE YEAR
THOMAS D. MOTTAZ
WORKERS' COMPENSATION LAW - CLAIMANTS
MINNEAPOLIS
2019

Best Lawyers
LAWYER OF THE YEAR
JERRY SISK
WORKERS' COMPENSATION LAW CLAIMANTS
MINNEAPOLIS
2021

STAR TRIBUNE READERS' CHOICE
MINNESOTA'S Best
2022 GOLD WINNER

Rated by
Super Lawyers
2023
visit SuperLawyers.com

Google

Martindale-Hubbell
AV PREEMINENT 2022
5.0/5.0

Minnesota Monthly
2022 TOP LAWYERS IN MINNESOTA

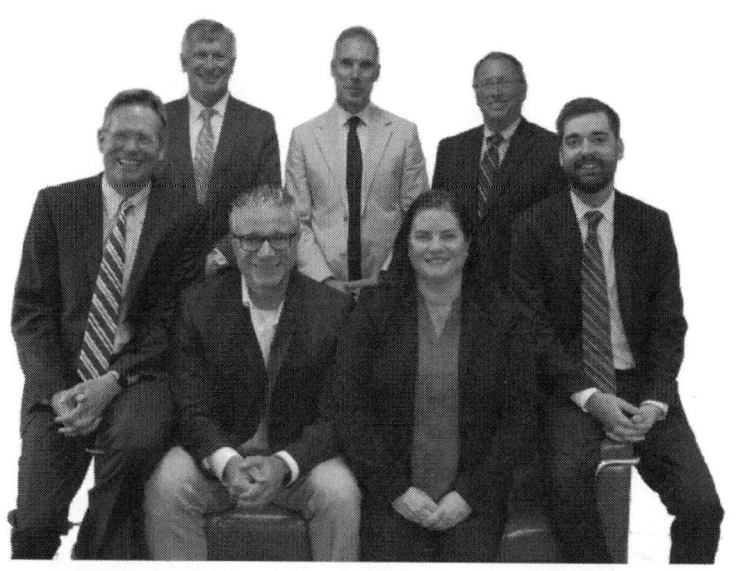

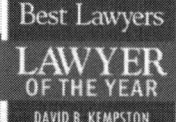

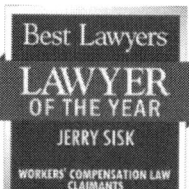

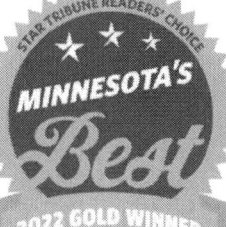

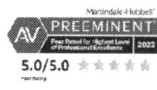

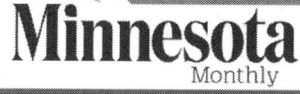

CONTENTS

From Mottaz & Sisk Injury Law 9

CHAPTER 1 11
MINNESOTA WORKERS' COMPENSATION 11
Minnesota Workers' Compensation Laws 11
Some Misperceptions of Workers' Compensation 12
Things To Do After A Work Injury 13
Importance of Reporting a Work Injury 17
Important Deadlines 18
Employer Obligations 18
Coverage for Workers' Compensation 19
Insurer Responsibility 20
Managed Care Programs/Plans and the Union Construction Workers' Compensation Program (MNUCWCP) 22

CHAPTER 2 25
MINNESOTA WORK INJURIES 25
Physical and Repetitive Trauma Injuries 25
Work-Related Injuries Off-Site 26
Mental or Psychological Injuries 27

CHAPTER 3 29
MINNESOTA WORKERS COMPENSATION BENEFITS 29
Medical Benefits 30
Wage Loss Benefits 32
    Temporary Disability Benefits 32

    Permanent Total Disability Benefits............................33
    Permanent Partial Disability 34
    Vocational Rehabilitation Benefits 36
    Retraining 37
    Death and Dependency Benefits 38
    Remodeling 39
    Cost of Living Increases 40
    Benefits Not Covered 40

CHAPTER 4 41
DEALING WITH THE ADJUSTER..41
    Trusting the Adjuster 42
    Recorded Statement 42
    Medical Authorizations and Forms 43
    Adjuster's Settlement Offer... 43

CHAPTER 5.. 45
NEEDING A LAWYER...45
    Problems with Your Claim 45
    Reasons to Speak to a Lawyer 46
    Hiring an Attorney... 47
    When an Attorney is Necessary 48
    Representing Yourself...51
    The Benefits of Hiring a Lawyer 51
    Fees and Costs for a Workers' Compensation Lawyer........53

CHAPTER 6 55
CONFERENCES, MEDITATIONS AND HEARINGS 55
    DOLI and OAH 55
    Workers Compensation Conferences and Hearings.......... 56
    Mediations 57

CHAPTER 7 59
INDEPENDENT MEDICAL EXAMINATIONS OR ADVERSE EXAMINATIONS 59

CHAPTER 8 63
SETTLEMENT 63
- The Value of your Case 64
- Expert Opinions Supporting Your Case 64
- The Type of Settlement 65
- Other Factors to Consider 65
- How Much to Ask For? 66
- Settlement Paperwork 66
- Vacating a Past Stipulation for Settlement 67

CHAPTER 9 69
FREQUENTLY ASKED QUESTIONS ABOUT THE WORKERS' COMPENSATION LITIGATION PROCESS 69
- What happens after an Employee's Claim Petition is filed? 69
- What is a deposition? 70
- Can the insurer require me to be seen by their doctor? 70
- What is an intervenor? 71
- What is a workers' compensation settlement? 71
- What is a hearing and what can I expect? 72
- Should I settle my case or go to a hearing? 72
- Can I sue my employer directly other than for workers' compensation benefits? 73

CHAPTER 10 77
GLOSSARY OF TERMS 77

CHAPTER 11 87
CONCLUSION 87

CHAPTER 12 89
FORMS 89
   Important Phone Numbers 89
   Mileage and Parking Form 91
   Job Logs 92

FROM MOTTAZ & SISK INJURY LAW

THANK YOU FOR for reading our guide! Our firm is dedicated to making a real difference for real people. Although no one ever expects to get injured at work, it is important workers understand their rights and know what to do if they get injured.

If you or someone you care about has recently been injured on the job, chances are you are worrying about what to do next. You may also feel angry, frustrated or wonder if there is a simple way to handle your unfortunate situation.

This guide goes through the basics of Workers' Compensation in Minnesota. Workers' Compensation law is different from state to state. Minnesota law is different than other states. You should be careful about what you read on the internet – the information you find may not apply to your situation. Speaking with an experienced workers' compensation attorney about your case is the best way to get the advice that will help YOU.

This guide also covers helpful topics and questions such as: What is Workers' Compensation? What benefits could be available to you? What is the timeline of a case? Each case is different. Your specific circumstances may not be outlined here and you should always consult with a workers' compensation attorney to get answers that are specific to you.

The purpose of this guide is to provide injured workers good, solid information about workers' compensation before they hire an attorney or deal with an insurance company. As we will point out later, not every case needs a lawyer. We truly believe, however, that you should have this valuable information right now, for free, before you are pressured by an insurance adjuster to answer questions or to settle your case.

Our motto is: Be empowered. Be educated. We want you to be better educated about the workers' compensation system so that you do not fall victim to the big insurance companies or self-insured employers.

This Guide is Not Legal Advice.

Even though we know the arguments the big insurance companies are likely to make in your claim, we are not providing you with legal advice in this book. This book is a reference guide to workers' compensation and we offer suggestions and identify certain pitfalls and traps, but the information in this guide is NOT legal advice. Your situation is unique and we can only give you proper legal advice specific to you once we agree, in writing, to work together on your case. In the meantime, please use this guide to become educated and become empowered.

For more information, visit our website at
www.mottazsiskinjurylaw.com

CHAPTER 1
MINNESOTA WORKERS' COMPENSATION

WORKERS' COMPENSATION IS a no-fault system designed to provide benefits to employees injured as a result of their employment activities and to limit the liability of employers. Because it is a no-fault system, the employee does not need to prove negligence or wrong-doing by the employer to establish liability. It also means the employer cannot use negligence or wrongdoing by the employee as a defense to a claim.

A work-related injury can be almost any condition that is caused, aggravated or accelerated by employment activities such as traumatic injuries, gradual injuries or occupational diseases. The employee need only show that the employment activities were a substantial contributing factor to the disability and/or need for medical care.

Every employer is liable for compensation in every case of personal injury or death of an employee arising out of, and in the course of, employment without regard to the question of negligence.

Minnesota Workers' Compensation Laws
While Minnesotans are known for being able to drive through the most treacherous weather conditions without batting an eyelash, they are not immune to workplace injuries and illnesses

once they actually get to work. Therefore, the state requires employers to purchase workers' compensation insurance, which covers work-related injuries and illnesses regardless of fault. If you have been injured while at work in Minnesota, you will want to understand the process for pursuing workers' compensation in Minnesota.

Some Misperceptions of Workers' Compensation

1. After an injury, I can seek medical treatment where I want.

USUALLY TRUE. The injured worker generally possesses the right to choose the treating doctor after a work injury. It has long been the law that Minnesota employees are given great latitude both in choosing and changing physicians.

However, this choice can be limited if the employer participates in a certified managed care plan. See section on Managed Care Programs and the Minnesota Union Construction Workers' Compensation Program (MNUCWCP). If that is the case, the employee will be required to pick a physician from the list provided by the plan – unless a documented history of treatment before the injury with that doctor can be demonstrated. Absent a certified plan, however, the employee has the right to choose which doctor will treat the injury.

2. I can collect money for my pain and suffering from my injury.

FALSE. The Minnesota workers' compensation law does NOT allow workers to collect money for pain and suffering.

3. The employer said it was my fault I got injured and that I cannot recover workers' compensation benefits.

USUALLY FALSE. Workers' compensation is a no-fault system. The accident can be 100% your fault and, as a general rule, you still can be entitled to full benefits under the Minnesota Workers' Compensation Act. However, there are some exceptions that could apply to your situation and talking to a lawyer is the best way to make sure you have the correct information.

4. The employer said it was my fault I got injured and that I cannot recover workers' compensation benefits.

FALSE. The only time an injured workers' ability to make a claim for benefits ends is if a Compensation Judge has found that an injury resolved or if the injured worker has signed a Stipulation for Settlement that has been approved by a Compensation Judge. In Minnesota, workers' compensation benefits can potentially be available for the rest of the injured workers' life regardless of whether they are still employed with the date of injury employer.

Things To Do After A Work Injury

Most employees do not know what to do when they have an on-the-job injury. It can become a very complicated and stressful situation. Consequently, it is a good idea to know what your injured worker's rights are under Minnesota workers' compensation law. These are things every injured worker should do following an injury.

1. Get Medical Treatment.

If you have been hurt on the job, the first thing you should do is seek medical attention. Once you get medical treatment, you must be mindful of how you move forward. For example, when you go to see a doctor, you should tell the doctor that you are receiving treatment for a work-related injury or condition. This way, the clinic or hospital will know to send the bill to your employer. Also, insist that medical benefits be paid by the employer's workers' compensation insurer rather than the employer group medical carrier.

It is also best to give your employer the name of the doctor and the address of the hospital that was used for treatment. In most cases, the employer or its insurer will also request past medical records. This information is used by the employer or insurer to determine whether they will accept your claim for workers' compensation benefits.

You have the right to choose which doctor you see. Keep in mind, if an employer sends you to a doctor and you see that doctor twice, that doctor then becomes your treating doctor. Therefore, make sure you choose your doctor wisely.

2. Report Your Injury Right Away.

Tell your supervisor immediately, or at least within 14 days, if you are injured at work. You risk losing your benefits altogether if you do not tell your employer within 180 days of your injury and give good reason for the delay.

After you have missed three days of work, your employer then has 10 days to submit a First Report of Injury to their insurance company who must then either deny your claim or begin making payments. Although verbal notice can be given to a supervisor under workers' compensation case law, this presents problems. The employer may later deny that there was any conversation about the work-related accident. If notice is given in writing, or if there are witness statements from a worker, the employer cannot then later deny that notice was given or that an accident occurred. *Always attempt to give some form of written notice.*

The employer is required to provide the injured worker with an informational sheet on workers' compensation rights that will be part of the First Report of Injury form. Call us if your employer refuses to let you report a work-related injury or suggests that you run a work-related medical expense through your insurance. This conduct can result in a fine being assessed against the employer by the State.

Try to Obtain a Witness Statement

A sample witness statement form is shown below. Whenever possible, always get a fellow employee to complete a short witness statement. People who have witnessed the accident or arrived at the scene shortly after the accident are in a good position to verify what happened and what they were told by you immediately after the accident. If your case goes to court, these witnesses can have a very powerful impact on the judge. Also, because most people tend to later forget important details, the sooner a witness statement is completed and signed the more your interests are protected.

SAMPLE WITNESS STATEMENT

I was a witness to an injury that was suffered by (name) _____ at (place) job site at _____. The injury occurred on or about (date) _____ at about (time)_____ The following is a brief summary of what I observed: (ex: John Smith slipped on a step as he was exiting his bulldozer and fell to the ground. I helped him get up, and he complained to me that his back hurt. He asked me to call the foreman.)

3. Be prepared.

We hope that people and insurance companies do the right thing and give you the benefits that you are owed under the law. However, that is not always the case. In workers' compensation, things can turn bad quickly. In other words, an insurance company that has been paying bills and wage loss benefits can suddenly stop paying – and this can happen even though you are still owed benefits. Thus, it is important to have an understanding of what benefits are available to you and what your legal options are in getting those benefits. *Speaking with an experienced workers' compensation lawyer is the best way to fully understand your options.*

NEVER GIVE A WRITTEN OR TELEPHONE STATEMENT TO AN INSURANCE CLAIMS REPRESENTATIVE IF THE COMPANY HAS ALREADY DENIED YOUR WORKERS' COMPENSATION CLAIM. Sometimes, an injured worker receives a notice of denial of benefits from the insurance company. The claims agent from the insurance company suggests they might reconsider, but the employee has to sign authorizations so the agent can talk to the treating doctor. The same agent may try to obtain a telephone statement that is recorded. In almost every case, the claims agent is not trying to help the injured worker, but is merely trying to dig up evidence of prior injuries or pre-existing conditions, which are then used against the injured worker. *You should immediately contact our office when you receive a written denial of your workers' compensation claim.*

4. Talk to a Lawyer.

Most lawyers in Minnesota, including the lawyers in our office, provide free consultations. Knowledge is power. Although you have a lot on your mind, talking to a knowledgeable and experienced attorney will be one of the best decisions you can make. Education is key, even if you wish this would all go away. Look out for yourself. One small slip-up in a workers' compensation claim can lead to no expenses being covered by your employer. There is never any obligation for you to sign up as a client, but you should be able to get your questions answered and learn your options.

Our office is happy to meet with potential clients either in person or over the phone to discuss their individual case.

Importance of Reporting a Work Injury

Reporting your injury to the employer is not just a formality, it is a legal requirement. Failure to report your injury in a timely fashion can result in an inability to get workers' compensation benefits. Regardless of whether the injury is a slip-and-fall, a herniated disc, or an injury from repetitive motion over time, you should always report your injury as soon as possible to the employer.

To receive workers' compensation benefits, injured workers must show they provided notice of the injury to the employer, or that the employer had actual knowledge of the injury, within 180 days. This does not require that you fill out any paperwork or a First Report of Injury, but instead, that you provided notice either verbally or in written form to the employer.

Notice must be given when it becomes "reasonably apparent" that an injury has resulted in, or is likely to cause, a compensable disability. Oftentimes, with repetitive or cumulative trauma injuries, known as Gillette type injuries, this may be difficult to know when you may have sustained an injury. The law requires that notice does not have to be given until the injured worker, as a reasonable person, should recognize the nature, seriousness and probable compensable character of their injury or disease. In other words, if you believe that you have a work-related injury – you report it.

Important Deadlines

As stated above, workers' compensation has a number of deadlines. Under Minnesota law, these deadlines have to be met. Failure to meet them can be a bar to future benefits. This means you cannot recover workers' compensation benefits for that injury.

- 4 days to report the injury to the employer to receive maximum benefits; under limited circumstances you may have up to 180 days to report your injury.

- **Statute of Limitations**: You have **3 years** after an injury to file a claim for benefits if no benefits have been paid and a First Report of Injury has been filed with the Department of Labor and Industry.

- **Statute of Limitations:** You have **6 years** after an injury to file a claim for benefits if no benefits have been paid, and a First Report of Injury has **NOT** been filed with the Department of Labor and Industry.

Employer Obligations

While injured workers' have a number of obligations when it comes to receiving benefits, so do employers.

- All employers are required to purchase workers' compensation insurance or obtain approval for self-insurance (with limited exceptions). Even if the employer closes their doors the workers' compensation insurer is still required to provide coverage.

- Employers have the right to choose the medical provider for the employee in limited cases such as Managed Care Programs. Otherwise, the injured worker is allowed to choose a medical provider.

- If an employee suffers a compensable injury and the employer <u>has not</u> purchased workers' compensation insurance, the employee may request the state's Special Compensation Fund pay benefits. The Special Compensation Fund will seek a penalty in the amount of 65 percent of those benefits against the employer.

- If a workers' compensation insurer goes bankrupt in certain circumstances the Minnesota Insurance Guaranty Association (MIGA) or the date of injury employer would be responsible for payment of benefits.

Coverage for Workers' Compensation

Minnesota has strict workers' compensation laws in that all employers must have workers' compensation insurance even if they have only one part-time employee. And most people who perform paid services for another are considered employees -- even minors and non-citizens -- though some types of workers are not automatically covered, such as independent contractors, volunteers, etc. Injuries that are caused, substantially aggravated, or accelerated by employment activities are also covered by workers' compensation insurance.

Insurer Responsibility

If the insurer **accepts** your claim for benefits:

- The insurer <u>must</u> send you a copy of the Notice of Insurer's Primary Liability Determination form stating your claim is accepted.

- The insurer <u>must</u> start paying wage-loss benefits within 14 days of the day your employer was informed about your work injury and lost wages.

- The insurer <u>must</u> pay wage loss benefits at the same intervals you were paid wages. See Chapter 3.

If the insurer **denies** your claim for benefits:

- The insurer <u>must</u> send you a copy of the Notice of Insurer's Primary Liability Determination form stating denial of primary liability for your claim. The form must clearly explain the facts and reasons the insurer is using to deny your claim.

- If denied, an injured worker should discuss their options with an experienced workers' compensation attorney.

Following a work injury, the workers' compensation insurer is prohibited from doing the following:

- Failing to reply, within 30 calendar days after receipt, to all written communication about a claim from a claimant that requests a response;

- Failing, within 45 calendar days after receipt of a written request, to commence benefits or to advise the claimant of the acceptance or denial of the claim by the insurer;

- Failing to pay or deny medical bills within 45 days after the receipt of all information requested from medical providers that is necessary to make a payment determination;

- Filing a denial of liability for workers' compensation benefits without conducting an investigation;

- Failing to regularly pay weekly benefits in a timely manner as prescribed by rules adopted by the commissioner once weekly benefits have begun. Failure to regularly pay weekly benefits means failure to pay an employee on more than three occasions in any 12-month period within three business days of when payment was due;

- Advising a claimant not to obtain the services of an attorney or representing that payment will be delayed if an attorney is retained by the claimant;

- Altering information on a document to be filed with the department without the notice and consent of any person who previously signed the document and who would be adversely affected by the alteration;

- Providing fraudulent written information to the department or an employee pertaining to a workers' compensation matter.

An injured worker may be entitled to penalties if an insurer violates any of the above.

Managed Care Programs/Plans and the Union Construction Workers' Compensation Program (MNUCWCP)

Some employers participate in a workers' compensation certified managed care plan or program. A certified managed care plan is an organization that has been certified by the state to manage health care for injured workers. An employer must tell an employee if they are covered by a certified managed care plan. Some employers or insurers may have contracted with a managed care plan or network of doctors who are not certified by the department.

There are only three managed care plans certified to provide managed care for services for an injury or condition covered under Minnesota Workers' Compensation.
1. Corvel
2. GENEX Services, Inc.
3. HealthPartners

An injured worker may be entitled to penalties if an insurer violates any of the above.

- Your employer must post a notice that shows how to get treatment using the managed care plan and provide the same and phone number of a contact person;

- You may ask the employer, the insurer or the certified managed care plan staff for a list of providers in the plan; and

- A medical case-manager might be assigned to coordinate the delivery of health care for your injury.

You must go to a provider in the certified managed care plan unless:

- You need emergency medical care;

- You want to receive care from another health care provider who is able to treat your injury and has treated you at least twice in the past two years or who has a documented history of treating you; or

- You live or work too far from a health care provider in the plan. (There is a 30-mile limit in the seven-county Twin Cities area and a 50-mile limit in all other areas.)

The Union Construction Program (UCWCP) is slightly different than the managed care programs as they not only direct which doctors you can see, but they also require you to utilize their dispute resolution system to obtain disputed benefits.

If you are an employee covered by the UCWCP:

- You must seek treatment within the Exclusive Provider Organization. This organization will include physicians who can treat work injuries;

- You may continue to treat with a physician if they previously performed surgery on the injured body part;

- You may trat with a physician one time who has previously provided treatment to that body part in order to obtain a referral;

- You may seek medical treatment with a facility outside the Exclusive Provider Organization (EPO) for emergency care. Follow-up care must be with a physician within the EPO.

This program is to be used in place of administrative conferences, settlement conferences, hearing and review processes conducted by the Department of Labor and Industry and Office of Administrative Hearings of the State of Minnesota. If a dispute arises over benefits in the UCWCP, a party can request a facilitation, a mediation or an arbitration.

If your injury is governed by one of these plans, it is important to understand how you can get benefits if they are denied. *Contact our office to speak with an experienced attorney to about your case.*

CHAPTER 2
MINNESOTA WORK INJURIES

AS LONG AS you are an "employee" and the injury is job-related, including broken bones, strains and sprains, herniated or bulging discs, or a substantial aggravation of a pre-existing medical condition, the injury is covered and you are entitled to workers' compensation benefits.

Physical and Repetitive Trauma Injuries

Workers' compensation covers every type of physical injury, including, but not limited to:

- Neck, back, shoulder, arm and hand injuries, including fractures, strains and sprains, herniated and bulging discs;

- Knee, leg and foot injuries, including fractures, strains and muscle tears;

- Nerve damage;

- Brain injuries (from head trauma and other causes);

- Repetitive injuries such as carpal tunnel syndrome ;

- Hearing loss as the result of exposure to loud noises at work;

- Amputation or loss of use of a body part;

- Burns;

- Occupational diseases, including asthma, asbestosis, mesothelioma and conditions resulting from exposure to chemicals and poisons;

- Repetitive injuries or <u>Gillette</u> injuries. Compensation is allowed for injuries that occur as a result of repetitive or cumulative trauma brought about by the performance of ordinary job duties. These injuries are called "<u>Gillette</u>" injuries. As a general rule, a <u>Gillette</u> injury culminates when the cumulative effect of repetitive trauma is sufficiently serious to disable the employee from further work;

- Death.

Work-Related Injuries Off-Site

A work-related injury is one that happened while you were doing something on behalf of your employer in the course of employment. Most injuries that can be classified as work-related are those that occur at the workplace. However, injuries can also occur in company-owned vehicles or at other locations as long as the employee was doing something connected to the job at the time of the injury. This can even include injuries while working remotely at home.

For example, an injuries may occur at employer sponsored social events or work activities that are not necessarily on company-owned property. Traveling employees may also be covered.

Compensable injuries under workers' compensation can sometimes include those resulting from "horseplay" or other instances where employees may have been disregarding workplace safety rules. Injuries that happen during lunch breaks may be considered work-related if they happen at the company cafeteria, on employer-owned grounds, or are otherwise connected to the course of employment, like lunch with a client at a restaurant.

Mental or Psychological Injuries

Under Minnesota law, only certain mental injuries are compensable including mental/physical and physical/mental. However, mental/mental injuries are not compensable unless it is diagnosed as Post Traumatic Stress Disorder or PTSD. The law differentiates between mental injuries and places them into three categories.

Mental/Physical – This means the mental injury causes a physical injury (i.e. heart attacks, ulcers, GERD, etc.). The employee must produce evidence that stress was extreme or beyond the day-to-day stress experienced by all employees. There must also be medical support linking the stress to the injury.

Physical/Mental – This means the physical injury causes the mental injury (i.e. consequential depression). Where a work-related physical injury causes, aggravates, accelerates, or precipitates a mental injury, that mental injury is compensable.

Mental/Mental – This means where the mental stimulus causes a mental injury (i.e. PTSD, anxiety caused by stressors at work, nervous breakdown). Typically, these claims are not compensable. However, in certain circumstances PTSD is covered.

For injuries occurring on or after October 1, 2013, PTSD can be a compensable workers' compensation injury if it arises out of and in the course of employment. To be compensable, PTSD must be diagnosed by a licensed psychiatrist or psychologist and must meet the description of PTSD in the most recent edition of the Diagnostic and Statistical Manual of Mental Disorders published by the American Psychiatric Association. PTSD is not considered a personal injury if it results from a disciplinary action, work evaluation, job transfer, layoff, demotion, promotion, termination, retirement or similar action taken in good faith by the employer.

Under the law, certain professions such as first responders, licensed police officers, firefighters, paramedics, emergency medical technicians, licensed nurses employed to provide emergency medical services outside of a medical facility, public safety dispatchers, officers employed by the state or a political subdivision at a corrections or detention facility, sheriffs and full-time deputy sheriffs of any county, and members of the Minnesota State Patrol are presumed to have a work related PTSD diagnosis if it is made following an incident that occurred while the employee is on active duty in one of the covered positions with no prior diagnosis of PTSD.

It may not always be clear as to whether your particular injury is covered or even technically work-related, so speaking with a workers' compensation attorney is a good idea.

CHAPTER 3
MINNESOTA WORKERS COMPENSATION BENEFITS

AFTER AN ACCIDENT, it is important to speak with an experienced workers' compensation lawyer who understands the various types of compensation benefits that are available and who can calculate the full value of each type of compensation you are eligible to receive

Although the law controls the specific amounts, duration and types of benefits in effect at the time of the injury, there are only certain types of Minnesota workers compensation benefits available to an injured worker.

In Minnesota, injured workers receive medical treatment, disability payments, and other valuable benefits through workers' compensation. Your benefits will vary depending on the date of injury, nature of your claim, your wages, and other factors. This book helps to explain how workers' compensation benefits are calculated in Minnesota.

The following types of benefits are available through workers' compensation in Minnesota:

- **Medical care**: all reasonable and necessary medical treatment or supplies required to treat the injury, including necessary travel expenses.

- **Wage-loss**: benefits for a percentage of income loss due to disability (temporary or permanent; partial or total). These are not taxed.

- **Vocational rehabilitation**: services and training if you cannot return to your job or employer, or if you require modifications to your current job, or if a surviving spouse needs training to become self-supporting.

- **Death benefits**: for burial costs, spouse, and dependents of an employee who dies from a work-related injury or disease.

- **Remodeling**: If an injured worker is permanently and totally disabled, they may be entitled to home remodeling of their principal residence.

- **Civil Action**: An injured worker may have a cause of action under Minn. Stat. §176.82 if terminated for a work injury.

You cannot receive workers' compensation until you make a claim for Minnesota workers' compensation benefits. If you need help with the claims process, contact a workers' compensation lawyer for assistance.

Medical Benefits

The employer and insurer are responsible for payment of causally related and "reasonable and necessary" medical treatment, which will aid in curing or relieving the effects of your work injury. Covered Minnesota workers comp medical treatments may include hospitalization, surgery, physical therapy, occupational therapy, chiropractic services, injection therapy, chronic pain management and many other forms of medical care. The right to receive these benefits may be impacted by the Minnesota Workers' Compensation Treatment Parameters depending on various factors including whether the injury is admitted or denied.

The health care provider, if it wants to get paid, must submit an itemized statement of charges on the prescribed billing form to the workers' compensation insurer within 60 days of the service and submit copies of medical records or reports that substantiate the nature of the charge and its relationship to the work injury.

A health care provider cannot attempt to collect or initiate any action for collection of the charge from any party until the information required has been furnished.

If the insurer has denied primary liability, the health care provider can bill the employee.

If the employee's health insurance pays the medical expenses, the insurance company has a right to reimbursement if it is later determined the charges are due to a compensable injury.

Medical treatment also includes mileage to and from the appointments. This is paid at the IRS mileage rate for that year. It is typically reimbursable every 30 days but has to be submitted by the injured worker.

If an injured worker is in need of at-home nursing or home health aide services, workers' compensation may be responsible for payment of those services.

The following items are allowed under the treatment parameters: braces, corsets, cervical collars, splints, TENS units, traction devices and exercise equipment (in conjunction with a chronic management program). The following items are not allowed under the treatment parameters: whirlpools, Jacuzzis, hot tubs, special bath or shower attachments, beds, waterbeds, mattresses, chairs, recliners and lounges.

Wage Loss Benefits

Temporary Disability Benefits

Temporary disability benefits cover a portion of your lost wages while you are recovering from your injuries. Benefits are paid once you have been off work for more than three days. (If your disability lasts for ten days, you will be retroactively paid for these first three days.) Benefits are paid until the insurer files a Notice of Intention to Discontinue Benefits or NOID.

Temporary total disability "TTD". If you are completely unable to work, you can receive temporary total disability (TTD) benefits or if the employer cannot accommodate your restrictions. TTD benefits are two-thirds of your average weekly wage, subject to a maximum and minimum weekly amount set by law. As of October 1, 2022, you will not receive more than $1,312.74 or less than $262.55 per week. See for the most uptodate:

https://www.dli.mn.gov/sites/default/files/pdf/annladj.pdf

TTD benefits are paid for a maximum of 130 weeks, unless the insurance company approves job retraining. TTD is paid until you return to work, no longer have restrictions or are at Maximum Medical Improvement (MMI).

Temporary partial disability "TPD". If you can return to work, but you are earning less than you usually do because of your work-related restrictions, you can receive temporary partial disability. TPD benefits are two-thirds of the difference between your pre-injury and post-injury wages (up to the state's maximum benefit). For example, if your AWW was $800, but now you can only earn $200, you would get $400 in TPD benefits ($800 - $200 = $600; 0.6666 x $600 = $400). TPD benefits are limited to either 225 weeks of paid benefits or 450 weeks post-injury (whichever comes first) for injuries before October 1, 2018. For injuries after October 1, 2018, the maximum number of weeks that an employee is entitled to increased from 225 to 275 weeks.

Permanent Total Disability Benefits

Once your doctors determine you are at MMI, and are unable to to return to work, you may be eligible for permanent total disability benefits. In Minnesota, permanent total disability (PTD) benefits are paid at two-thirds of your average weekly wage. This would be the benefit owed if you could not return to work ever again.

The state's maximum benefit applies to PTD claims and Minnesota sets a maximum and minimum PTD benefit. State law presumes that you are totally and permanently disabled if you:

- lose all use of both arms, eyes, feet, hands, or legs,

- suffer complete and permanent paralysis, or

- are completely mentally disabled.

If you meet any of these criteria, PTD benefits must be paid even if you return to work.

Other injuries and occupational illnesses may also be permanently and totally disabling. However, you must meet additional thresholds, based on your age and education. These thresholds include:

- **49 years old or younger**: 17 percent permanent partial disability rating (see below for a discussion of impairment ratings)

- **50 years or older**: at least a 15 percent impairment rating, or

- **55 years or older without a high school diploma or a GED**: at least a 13 percent impairment rating.

If you meet these criteria, and if based on your age, disability and transferable skills there is no substantial gainful employment in your labor market, your PTD benefits are paid to the age of 67 unless you can prove you were not planning to retire before then.

For injuries after October 1, 2018, the retirement presumption changed to age 72. There is an exception provided for employees who are injured after age 67, whose permanent total disability benefits will cease after five years.

Permanent Partial Disability

If your doctor finds that you suffer permanent loss or impairment or loss of function, you may be eligible for permanent partial disability (PPD) benefits. Instead of paying a set amount for certain body parts, like some states do, Minnesota assesses how much you have lost of your total body function. Once you reach MMI, your doctor will give you a total body impairment rating, stated as a percentage. This is based on the Minnesota Workers' Compensation Permanency Schedule under Minnesota Rule

5223. This is not payable until your TTD benefits have stopped and is payable in a lump sum or paid out weekly.

Your PPD rate is not based on your average weekly wage, unlike most other workers' compensation benefits. Instead, Minnesota law has a compensation schedule. Your impairment rating is multiplied by the scheduled award. For dates of injury through at least 2023, the compensation schedule includes:

PPD	Before 10/1/18	10/1/18 to 9/30/23	After 10/1/23
0 to less than 5.5 %:	$75,000	$78,800	$114,260
5 to less than 10.5 % :	$80,000	$84,400	$121,800
11 to less than 15.5 %:	$85,000	$89,300	$129,485
16 to less than 20.5 %	$90,000	$94,500	$137,025
21 to less than 25.5 % :	$95,000	$99,800	$139,720
26 to less than 30.5%:	$100,000	$105,000	$147,000
31 to less than 35.5%:	$110,000	$115,500	$150,150
36 to less than 40.5%:	$120,000	$126,000	$163,800
41 to less than 45.5%:	$130,000	$136,500	$177,450
46 to less than 50.5%:	$140,000	$147,000	$177,870
51 to less than 55.5%:	$165,000	$173,300	$181,965
56 to less than 60.5%:	$190,000	$199,500	$209,475
61 to less than 65.5%:	$215,000	$225,800	$237,090
66 to less than 70.5%:	$240,000	$252,000	$264,600
71 to less than 75.5%:	$265,000	$278,300	$292,215
76 to less than 80.5%:	$315,000	$330,800	$347,340
81 to less than 85.5%:	$365,000	$383,300	$402,464
86 to less than 90.5%:	$415,000	$435,800	$457,590
91 to less than 95.5%:	$465,000	$488,300	$512,715
96 to less than 100.5%:	$515,000	$540,800	$567,840

Example: If you have a 35 percent impairment rating before 10/1/18, you will receive a total PPD benefit of $38,500 ($110,000 x 0.35 = $38,500). PPD benefits can be paid either over time or in a lump sum. If you choose a lump sum, your award may be reduced up to five percent

If you disagree with your impairment rating or need help understanding your PPD benefit amounts, contact an experienced Minnesota workers' compensation lawyer. A lawyer can evaluate your claim and, if necessary, help get you the correct rating.

Vocational Rehabilitation Benefits

Vocational rehabilitation benefits are designed to assist the injured worker returning to their former employment or to a job related to that employment. In the alternative, rehabilitation services assist the injured employee to return to a job in another work area, which produces an economic status as close as possible to that enjoyed but for the disability. This assistance may include direct job placement, on-the-job training or formal retraining. Rehabilitation services can include the use of a Qualified Rehabilitation Consultant ("QRC") to help with medical management, return to work, and job placement.

Retraining includes a formal course of study which is designed to return you to suitable gainful employment. The maximum duration is 156 weeks. Vocational retraining is to be given equal consideration with other rehabilitation services, and proposed for approval if other considered services are not likely to lead to suitable gainful employment such as job placement services.

Retraining

You can make a request for vocational retraining by discussing the matter with your QRC or Qualified Rehabilitation Consultant. The QRC would then work with you in preparing a formal retraining plan to be submitted to the Minnesota Department of Labor and Industry. It must be approved by the State of Minnesota in order for you to be allowed to be retrained. It may also be to your benefit to discuss the matter with an experienced attorney who has been successful in getting retraining plans approved. Often, the injured worker has only one opportunity to get retrained. Failure to take the appropriate steps could potentially cause a retraining plan not to be approved.

Will the retraining plan cover my books, tuition, mileage, and wages?

If the retraining plan is approved, the insurer will cover your books, tuition, mileage and wages, while you are enrolled in the program. Wage replacement benefits are paid, even covered, regardless of whether you have used up all or even a portion of your temporary partial or temporary total disability benefits available to you. However, they are limited to 156 weeks. The insurer may also be responsible for other items such as laptops or computers if required as part of the course of study. Daycare may also be a covered expense.

When Must a Claim for Retraining be made?

It is important to discuss with an attorney your rights to retraining and whether you are a retraining candidate. Failure to make a request for retraining before the below deadlines could be a bar to retraining benefits.

- If your date of injury is from Oct. 1, 1995, through Sept. 30, 2000, you must file your request for retraining benefits before 104 weeks of wage-loss benefits have been paid to you.

- If your date of injury is from Oct. 1, 2000, through Sept. 30, 2008, you must file your request for retraining benefits before 156 weeks of wage-loss benefits have been paid to you.

- If you were injured on or after Oct. 1, 2008, you must file your request for retraining before 208 weeks of wage-loss benefits have been paid to you.

What if the workers compensation insurer is denying my request for retraining?

Contact our office and speak with a lawyer right away. Our office has been extremely successful in getting retraining plans approved. Our office can assist in filing a rehabilitation request and making sure the appropriate measures are taken to get you retraining.

Death and Dependency Benefits

If an injury or illness results in death, the worker's spouse and dependents may receive weekly death benefits. It is always a tragic situation when someone dies from a work-related injury. However, you should be rest assured that dependency benefits are available.

Dependency benefits are based upon weekly wage and daily wage which is determined by the hours normally worked in that employment. Benefits are paid to the spouse, children, or dependents. These benefits can be paid out weekly until a minor child completes schooling and, at times, even up to 10 years more for a spouse. Allocation amongst the various individuals depends on the type and number of dependents the decedent had at his/her death.

The minimum amount of dependency benefits that must be paid is $60,000. When there are no persons entitled to monetary benefits, the estate of the injured worker is to be paid $60,000.

Additionally, the insurance company must pay up to $15,000 for the worker's reasonable funeral and burial expenses.

If a fatal accident occurs, contact our office immediately to review your rights.

Remodeling

If an injured worker is permanently and totally disabled, they may be entitled to home remodeling of their principal residence. In other words, they would need to own the home. Benefits are limited to a maximum of $30,000 for injuries that occur prior to October 1, 1992 and up to $60,000 for injuries occurring from October 1, 1992 to May 28, 2011. After 2011 the maximum limit increased to $75,000.

The intent of home remodeling is to allow the injured worker to be able to move freely into and throughout the residence and to otherwise adequately accommodate the disability.

It is important in any type of home remodeling case to determine the functional limitations of the injured worker to determine what alterations need to occur. A home assessment is also necessary. Any changes must be done under the supervision of a licensed architect and must be approved by the Minnesota Council on Disability.

If you or a loved one are seeking home remodeling it's important to discuss your case with an experienced workers' compensation lawyer.

Cost of Living Increases

Minnesota also requires cost of living increases after a period of time. The frequency and amount of your increase will vary, depending on your date of injury. An injured worker is eligible for their first cost of living adjustment (COLA) on the third anniversary of their injury. From then on, they will receive an annual COLA of up to three percent.

Benefits Not Covered

Workers' compensation is not designed to make the injured worker "whole." The legislature designed workers' compensation to have limited recoveries. Therefore, these benefits are not recoverable:

- Pain and Suffering;

- Loss of consortium;

- Emotional distress;

- Wages for lost insurance, 401k, pension, etc;

- Punitive damages.

CHAPTER 4
DEALING WITH THE ADJUSTER

WORKERS' COMPENSATION IS complex. As an injured worker, this is probably the first time you have dealt with complexities of workers' compensation law.

Your insurance adjuster, however, has dealt with these issues many times. Be careful that you know the law before you make any decisions or before you agree to anything the adjuster may tell you, including giving a recorded interview to the adjuster. Speaking with and possibly hiring an experienced workers' compensation lawyer can help ensure that your rights are protected.

After an injury at work, you will usually be contacted by an insurance adjuster. The adjuster works for the workers' compensation insurance company. Instead of using the term "adjuster", this person may refer to himself or herself as a case manager, claims representative or some other job title.

An insurance adjuster works for your employer's workers compensation insurance company. Their job is to investigate the facts and circumstances surrounding your claim, to determine whether your injuries are covered under the Minnesota Workers' Compensation Act, and to try to negotiate a workers compensation settlement with you.

You may receive a letter from the insurance adjuster. It may be a phone call or an email. Insurance adjusters will often ask you to provide information about your injury. They want you to sign documents authorizing them to get your medical records and other information.

You probably have questions. Should you trust this person? Do you have to provide this information? Here are some answers to some of those questions.

Trusting the Adjuster

The insurance adjuster works for the insurance company. The insurance company is a business that wants to make money. Your case costs them money. So, they generally want to try to pay you as little as possible.

This does not mean that the insurance adjuster is a bad person. In fact, the insurance adjuster may be a very nice person. But their job is usually to pay you as little as possible on your case. You should be very cautious about believing that they are your friend or that they are on your side. They are not on your side.

The workers' compensation claims adjuster does not have to give you guidance on how to maximize your legal rights after a work accident. In fact, they may not tell you about the benefits that are available to you. So you should be cautious when dealing with the adjuster and speak with an attorney who will let you know what you are entitled to for compensation.

Recorded Statement

You do not have to provide a recorded statement to the adjuster, and in fact, you should not without an attorney.

It is important to know that the adjuster is going to do an investigation of your injury. The adjuster usually makes the decision about whether to pay you workers' compensation benefits or deny your claim. The adjuster may want to take a statement as part of that investigation. That is fine so long as it is not a recorded statement.

It is also important to know that information you provide to the adjuster will be used to accept or to deny your claim. If you do decide to give a statement, be sure you tell the truth and be sure to carefully consider your answers. Many people get tripped up by rushing through a statement and leaving out something important.

Medical Authorizations and Forms

The insurance adjuster often will send you forms to sign. You should read over and carefully consider any forms before signing them.

The most common form that an adjuster will send you is a medical authorization. A medical authorization allows someone to get your medical records. Under Minnesota workers' compensation laws, you do have to provide the insurance company with a certain type of medical authorization when requested.

Adjuster's Settlement Offer

In many cases, it is not uncommon for workers' comp insurers to have adjusters contact claimants in an attempt to get them to settle their case early and on their own, oftentimes for much lower than what they actually deserve. This can be dangerous. Settling early can cause a person to be held financially liable for any future medical expenses or losses. Speak with an attorney first before accepting a settlement.

Again, adjusters are there to do their job – not to be your friend. Be honest, polite but always know they will do what is best for the insurance company, not you.

CHAPTER 5
NEEDING A LAWYER

One of the many things that our office prides ourselves on is giving good, ethical advice. This includes advising you whether you need an attorney or not. In some situations, if all your benefits are being paid and there are no issues, you may not need an attorney. However, if you are experiencing problems with your claim, or it is anticipated that a dispute will arise in the near future, it may be a situation where retaining an attorney can be the best decision you can make

Problems with Your Claim

If your claim is denied or there is a dispute regarding benefits, you do have options, including the following:

- Call the insurance claims adjuster and attempt to resolve the issue with them;

- Discuss the problem with an Alternative Dispute Resolution specialist at the Department of Labor and Industry (651)-284-5005; or

- Request a hearing or conference by filing an Employee's Claim Petition, Medical Request, Rehabilitation Request or Request an Administrative Conference (many employees choose to have an attorney help with preparing documents, meeting deadlines, and arguing their case during these proceedings)

- Contact a Lawyer. Denial of workers' compensation is a serious matter, but it is not a cause for panic. Injured workers can pursue their cases or request payment of benefits if benefits are reduced, limited or denied. By learning more about the system and how to prepare for it, you can protect your rights and the rights of your family. A Minnesota injury attorney can help you navigate through the process. We are experts with Minnesota's workers' compensation law and we provide a free claim evaluation on the strength and potential of your claim.

Reasons to Speak to a Lawyer

The adage is that the best time to talk to a lawyer is when you do not actually need one. Some of the reasons why you may want to speak to a lawyer include:

1. You Want to Be Empowered

A licensed lawyer that practices in workers' compensation can tell you about the applicable laws that apply to your case. Looking for information online may yield inaccurate or outdated information. A professional can provide current information and relevant information. I always tell people - after you have spoken with Lawyer Google, come talk to me. You will not always get the right information online.

2. You Want to Ease Your Mind

Not knowing is sometimes the worst feeling in the world. It is often better to know what you are facing even if this involves negative information. To remove the feeling of paralysis, many people consult with a lawyer to learn about their options.

3. You Need to Know Your Options

A lawyer can provide objective information about the options available in your case along with the pros and cons of each option.

4. You Want to Avoid Mistakes

While legal information is widely available on the Internet, this information is often not accurate. Even if the information is accurate, the law is a complex area that requires strict adherence to deadlines, filing requirements and procedures. Sometimes doing the work yourself can be much more expensive because then you must hire a lawyer to fix your mistakes.

Mottaz & Sisk Injury Law offers free consultations for injured workers and their families to discuss their legal options. We will spend as much time as needed to discuss your case.

Contact our office or calling 763.421.8226 or emailing at admin@mottazlaw.com.

Hiring an Attorney

Hiring the right worker's compensation attorney can make all the difference in your injury claim. The right attorney will fight to make sure all your medical benefits are covered and that you receive all of the lost time benefits you are entitled to under the Workers' Compensation Law.

Our attorneys are experts in the field of Minnesota workers' compensation. Our lawyers are litigators, professors, authors, and teachers of workers' compensation in Minnesota. We have been recognized as the best by SuperLawyers and US & News

World Report. We have received numerous accolades and awards for our work. We are the law firm that defense lawyers, judges, adjusters, doctors, professional athletes, etc. come to for their or their loved one's workers' compensation case.

When an Attorney is Neccesary

Typically, we are going to recommend you hire a workers' compensation lawyer when there is any real complexity introduced into your case. For example:

1. You have been denied benefits.

Your employer denies your claim or you fail to receive your benefits promptly. Employers and workers' comp insurers routinely reject bona fide workers' comp claims, confident that many workers will fail to follow-up. Unfortunately, they're usually correct. Up to 80% of individuals who are hurt at work simply accept the denial of their claim without further follow-up. Hiring a workers' compensation attorney costs nothing up front, and gives you the best chance to get compensation for your injuries.

2. You want to settle your case.

Your employer's settlement offer does not always cover all your lost wages or medical bills. If you are not sure your settlement offer is good enough, do not rely on the insurer to make sure that you are getting a fair deal. Although workers' compensation settlements must have judicial approval, judges will usually sign off on any agreement as long as it is not grossly unfair. If you really want someone to get you the best settlement possible, call an attorney.

3. You are not able to go back to work at all.

Your medical issues prevent you from returning to your prior job, or from performing any work at all. These types of cases can be monumentally expensive for insurance companies, and they will often stop at nothing to avoid paying you what you deserve. A knowledgeable workers' compensation attorney is essential in cases involving permanent injuries or illness.

4. You receive Social Security disability benefits.

If your workers' comp settlement is not structured properly, Social Security may offset a large portion of your benefits. An experienced attorney will understand how to draft your settlement agreement to minimize or eliminate this offset.

5. Your boss retaliates against you for filing a workers' compensation claim.

If your boss has fired you, demoted you, reduced your hours, reduced your pay, or engaged in any other form of discrimination because you filed a workers' compensation claim, contact a workers' compensation attorney immediately.

6. You have a third-party claim.

You may have a potential third-party claim depending on whether another party is at fault. Although the workers' compensation system was designed to keep work injury cases from the civil tort system, you are permitted to sue a third-party whose negligence contributed to your injury. For example, a delivery driver who is struck by a negligent motorist can file a civil suit against the motorist in addition to receiving workers' compensation benefits. Civil damages often exceed workers' compensation settlements because they account for non-economic harms such as pain and suffering.

Examples:

1. A manufacturer sells a defective power tool to Xcel Energy that shatters, blinding the worker who is using it.

2. A driver while making a delivery stop is injured in a fall from a broken step because the business failed to fix or warn of the problem.

3. A worker installing phones on a construction site is seriously injured when a temporary door/wall unit that is improperly installed by a general contractor collapses on him when he enters the building.

In all of these examples, the injured worker has a lawsuit over and above workers' compensation. The reason that both sets of benefits are necessary is that workers' compensation alone often fails to fully compensate a seriously injured worker for all his losses.

All seriously injured workers must determine their legal rights as soon as possible. If you have permanent restrictions that will prevent you from returning to your pre-injury occupation, you need a legal consult.

Call us, and we will discuss your rights without charge.

Representing Yourself

As a general rule, you may be able to get by without an attorney if all of the following statements are true:

- You suffered a minor workplace injury, such as a twisted ankle or a cut requiring a few stitches.

- You missed little or no work due to your injury.

- Your employer admits that the injury happened at work.

- You do not have a pre-existing condition.

Even in these relatively uncomplicated situations, it is often a good idea to contact a workers' compensation attorney for a free consultation about your case. The attorney can walk you through the process, alert you to potential pitfalls, and give you an honest appraisal of whether you can handle the case on your own.

The Benefits of Hiring a Lawyer

In addition, to making sure that you file the necessary forms and meet all deadlines, your attorney will understand how to develop medical evidence that documents the severity of your condition. Relying on the supposedly "independent" physicians who perform exams for insurance companies is a common but costly error committed by unrepresented claimants. Moreover, a workers' compensation attorney can estimate the "worth" of your case and evaluate any settlement offers much more accurately than your co-workers, friends, or family members can.

Selecting the Right Attorney

There are certain characteristics to look for in a lawyer, including the following:

1. A lawyer that primarily practices in the area of law that is the subject of your legal issue. Our office has expert attorneys in Minnesota workers' compensation. Our attorneys are frequent speakers on workers' compensation topics in Minnesota and have been recognized by Super Lawyers Magazine.

2. A lawyer who treats you with respect, listens to you and addresses your concerns.

3. A lawyer who explains the options available to you and the pros and cons of each one.

4. A lawyer whom you trust. You will work closely with the lawyer to resolve your legal issues, so it is important that you and the lawyer have a good rapport.

There are also characteristics and types of lawyers to avoid. These include:

1. A lawyer who makes a guarantee. No lawyer can absolutely ensure that they will win your case.

2. A lawyer with ethical issues. Avoid those who have had problems in the past in maintaining client

confidentiality and representing clients when there was an apparent conflict of interest or managing client funds.

3. A lawyer who advertises that they practice in all areas of the law. Many lawyers focus on a limited number of areas of the law to ensure that they have a working knowledge of the subject.

4. A lawyer who does not give you the attention you deserve, avoids phone calls and does not provide copies of requested information.

5. A lawyer who tries to settle your case right away. There are lawyers will do anything to earn a quick buck. Avoid these lawyers are all costs. Rarely, do they put in the work to appropriate advise you or prosecute your case

Picking the right lawyer will make a huge difference on the outcome of your case.

Fees and Costs for a Workers' Compensation Lawyer

There is no fee to meet with our attorneys to discuss your workers' compensation case. We do not charge a fee unless you retain our office and we are able to recover benefits on your behalf. **This means if you retain our office and during the life of your claim we do not recover any disputed or new benefits, you will not owe us anything**. We will monitor your case and make sure to advise you on important issues.

Minnesota workers' compensation attorney fees are handled on a contingency basis. No fee is owed unless we are able to recover additional workers' compensation benefits or a settlement. For injuries before October 1, 2013, attorney fees would be paid on a contingency basis of 25% of the first $4,000 recovered and 20% thereafter. After October 1, 2013, dates injuries, the law changed to 20% of workers' compensation benefits. In the case that there is no money paid directly to you, whether it be wage loss, permanency or a settlement, and in a situation where we recover medical or rehabilitation benefits on your behalf, we are allowed to have the insurance company pay our hourly fees.

Fees are different from costs. **We pay all the costs associated with your case**. Gathering medical records, obtaining narrative reports and taking depositions all cost money. We will never ask that you pay those costs. If we win your case, we get the insurance company to reimburse us. If we lose, you never pay. Please note that not every attorney in Minnesota does it this way. In fact, many may ask you to pay it back if they lose or if you fire them for not doing their job.

If you retain one of our attorneys, a retainer agreement will be provided to you outlining the fees and costs. This is required under the law. Once signed the lawyers will start working on your case. Again, meeting with one of Minnesota workers' compensation lawyers for an initial consultation is free with no obligation.

CHAPTER 6
CONFERENCES, MEDIATIONS AND HEARINGS

DOLI and OAH

Workers' compensation claims can be confusing, especially when you start to think about where the claim for benefits needs to be filed. Unlike civil cases, workers' compensation cases are handled administratively. This means they are going to have their own rules and regulations as to how litigated claims are handled.

Under Minnesota workers' compensation, there are two different places or venues where a disputed claim can be filed—Minnesota Department of Labor and Industry (DOLI) or the Minnesota Office of Administrative Hearings (OAH). (See page 88 for a flow chart) The type of document filed, and the nature of the dispute, will dictate where it will be heard. Typically, DOLI will hear issues of medical and rehabilitation under $7,500 if it is an admitted claim (ie. Benefits were paid). OAH will hear all other disputes including wage loss and disputes over $7,500 where claims are either admitted or denied. Documents that can be filed to recover benefits can include:

- Medical Requests

- Claim Petitions and

- Rehabilitation Requests.

Once a claim has been filed the employer and insurer have a right to conduct discovery which includes having the injured worker undergo what is called an Adverse Medical Examination commonly referred to as Independent Medical Examination (IME) although they are no independent. In certain cases, an employer and insurer may also request an Adverse Vocational Evaluation (AVE/IVE) if the injured worker claims that their ability to earn has been reduced by the injury. During the discovery process, the injured worker and her attorney are also afforded an opportunity to obtain records from the employer, conduct depositions of experts and relevant parties and request medical records before going to a hearing.

Workers Compensation Conferences and Hearings

Once the appropriate documents have been filed with the state a conference or hearing will be scheduled. The purpose of an administrative conference is to resolve issues regarding wage loss, medical and rehabilitation services. Administrative conferences are typically scheduled for a half hour to an hour and are less formal than a hearing as no sworn testimony is given and a formal record is not kept.

A hearing is the equivalent of a "trial" in civil cases. However, it is nothing like you see on TV. Instead, hearings are conducted at OAH, by video or at other designated locations throughout the state. There is no jury. Instead, a compensation judge will consider all the evidence. A hearing before the judges will be scheduled for either a half or a full day depending on the issues. The parties offer evidence and sworn testimony is given.

The parties are bound to follow certain rules when conducting themselves at a hearing.

Following the conclusion of the conference or hearing, the mediator or Judge will take the matter under advisement and issue a Decision and Order (DO) or a Findings and Order (FO), which can be appealed within 30 days. If it is an administrative decision (DO) any party can request a formal evidentiary hearing before a compensation judge. If it is a hearing it can be appealed to the Workers' Compensation Court of Appeals.

Mediations

A mediation is a way for all parties to get together and attempt to reach a settlement. Mediation is a non-binding process where all parties meet to discuss the disputed issues before a neutral mediator who is chosen by the lawyers. The mediator will help the parties reach a mutual settlement by exploring the strengths and weaknesses of each party. It is not the mediator's role to decide who is right or wrong but instead help the parties reach a fair and equitable settlement.

At the mediation, typically the defense lawyer will be in a different room so the injured worker should not be worried about confronting or dealing with the defense lawyer personally.

If the dispute resolves, typically a Stipulation for Settlement will be drafted to document the settlement. It will need to be approved by a Compensation Judge before the settlement can be finalized. See Chapter 8.

CHAPTER 7
INDEPENDENT MEDICAL EXAMINATIONS OR ADVERSE EXAMINATIONS

AS PART OF the legal procedures involved in a workers' compensation claim, the injured worker is often requested to go to an adverse medical examination. Under Minnesota workers' compensation, the injured worker must attend the medical examination set up to "adversely" examine him/her. The doctor you will be seeing for the adverse medical exam is hired by the insurance company. Sometimes, the doctor that they hire will be one of their "pet doctors" that they use in such cases. These doctors often find nothing wrong with people or little wrong with people with great consistency. On the other hand, sometimes they send you to doctors that are somewhat honest and they may even end up supporting your claim.

It is important that you attend the examination. If you cannot attend, you must let your attorney, or the other side know right away. The insurance company may look to discontinue your benefits if you miss the exam and has the right to charge you for the doctor's time. Sometimes, this can be as high as $1,500.

Examinations are scheduled at various times. In a workers' compensation claim, the insurance company is obligated to set an examination within 120 days following the filing of the Claim Petition. Usually, they will want to take your deposition prior to the adverse examination so they can provide the doctor with not only the previous medical records, but also your testimony as to previous injuries and the injury in question.

Those adverse examinations are usually scheduled no later several months after the date of the injury. Once you get to the examination, the doctor or staff member will take your history. This will consist of questions regarding what medical treatment or injuries you have had in the past. The doctor will then examine you and question you regarding your injuries and the history.

If you have an IME, you should follow the following instructions:

1. Make sure you wear a watch and time the amount of time that the doctor is in your physical presence. There are several adverse doctors who spend only five to eight minutes doing adverse examinations, no matter how complicated the case. Make sure you are accurate about the time the doctor spends with you.

2. Be careful and precise about what you tell the adverse medical doctor. The physician will be taking notes and anything you say may be used in the case.

3. Explain all of your medical concerns to the doctor doing the adverse medical examination, all your symptoms and complaints. Do not let the adverse doctor cut you off.

4. If you have any history of prior problems, be honest about it and make sure you tell the doctor when he asks about that. In these cases, all your medical records and

background comes to the surface sooner or later. Thus, not telling of any prior difficulties with your problem such as leaving out information about preexisting conditions or injuries will only make you look bad. It may also harm your case

5. Be polite to the doctor and do not argue.

6. Be honest in answering all questions asked by the doctor. This pertains to the examination as well. For example, I had one case where part of the examination involved a pin prick type test for numbness of a man's arm. He lied about having numbness and the doctor re-checked him and caught him. That does not help the case. Similarly, in a low back injury case straight leg raising to test leg nerve pressure can be done sitting and lying down. In past cases, some clients have complained of pain with very little movement of the leg when lying down, but when tested sitting do not complain.

7. If you have had symptoms in the past concerning your injury which have improved at the time you see the adverse doctor, make sure you tell the doctor about the symptoms in the past as well. This may be very important in that some symptoms traditionally reoccur after a period of remission. Good and bad days and good and bad periods often occur in orthopedic injury cases.

8. When you are done with your adverse medical examination, make written notes about the

examination, what the doctor did, what type of testing was performed and, especially, what the doctor said to you.

9. Do not be overly worried about the adverse medical examination. It is just one other procedure you must go through to get your case resolved. Sometimes it helps the resolution of the case.

Following the examination, the doctor will write a report to the insurance company describing the examination findings and opinions. They will send your attorney or you a copy. At times, the findings are consistent with the treating physicians regarding continued treatment and benefits owed for your physical condition. However, this is rare. Remember, they are working for the insurer. It is also encouraged that you bring a copy of the IME report to your treating physician for comment.

Lastly, keep track of any mileage related expenses incurred from the examination. You should then forward them to your attorney or adjuster for reimbursement.

CHAPTER 8
SETTLEMENT

AFTER A WORK-RELATED INJURY, there may come a time when either the insurance or you want to be done with your workers' compensation case. In this situation, a settlement could be reached whereby certain benefits are settled or closed out in exchange for a cash settlement or payment of certain benefits. The decision to settle can never be an easy decision to make. Many different factors need to be weighed into your decision. It is imperative that all your options have been discussed so that an informed decision can be made. When determining whether to settle your compensation case you should consider the following:

Minnesota Workers' Compensation Benefits Could be Payable for the Rest of Your Life

Unlike a personal injury or civil case, workers' compensation benefits can be ongoing for the rest of your life. Now, not all benefits are payable on an ongoing basis as there are caps and limits to certain types of benefits. However, benefits such as medical expenses will continue to be paid for the rest of your life so long as the treatment is reasonable, necessary and related to your injury. Additionally, wage loss benefits such as permanent total disability (PTD) can be paid until the age of 67 or even longer, in certain situations.

Things to Consider Before Settling

Value of your Case

In evaluating whether a settlement is reasonable or whether you should even consider settlement, you first need to keep in mind what benefits are available to you. In other words, understand what you are giving up. Once you know that you can then assess whether you will be needing those benefits in the future. Refer to Chapter 3 for more information.

Whether it is life insurance, health insurance, auto insurance, etc, there can be a good reason why you keep it intact – because you may need it. The same is true with workers' compensation insurance coverage for your injury. Again, unlike personal injury cases, your worker' compensation case could be open for the rest of your life. It is important to recognize what you may be giving up if you settle your case.

Expert Opinions Supporting Your Case

Another factor to consider is what type of support you have for your case. In other words, what are your doctors, physicians, and medical professionals saying about your case? Are the doctors saying that you are as good as you are going to get or are they saying that you may need future surgery? Are you back to work at full wages or is it unclear as to whether you will need to be retrained to get back to work? There are a lot of different questions that need to be asked and considered by doctors, physicians, and even QRCs to determine whether or not the settlement is right for you.

The Type of Settlement

You also need to decide on what type of settlement you want. Quite often, the insurance companies want to pay a sum of money for you to "go away" completely. This could even include future medical benefits. As a result, it is important to weigh your options as to whether a settlement on a "to-date" basis versus a settlement that will pay you more money, but you may close out any and all benefits in the future. Again, not every settlement is right for one type of case. You should consider all your options fully.

Other Factors to Consider

Additionally, there may be other factors to consider when settling your case including:

- Will my health insurance cover my future medical expenses?

- Will I have to resign from my job?

- Will I be able to afford future medical or wage loss?

- Will my medical bills be taken care of?

- Will I be able to find another job?

- Will I continue to have to fight for workers' compensation even after a settlement?

Every case is different, but it is important to discuss your case with an experienced workers' compensation attorney when deciding to settle your case.

How Much to Ask For?

Lastly, a decision needs to be made about what you request to be paid and what final number you are willing to walk away with. In discussing the money associated with settlement, all the above factors need to be taken into account and weighed to make an appropriate determination as to the appropriate settlement. Other factors may also be weighed.

Recently, the Department of Labor and Industry performed a survey of injured workers after they had gone to trial or settled their case. Less than 20% felt that they had improved, while 35%-45% felt that there was no change, and 40%-45% felt that they got worse after they finished their case.

Settlement is a difficult choice that should not be taken lightly. Discussing the matter fully with an attorney is always a good option.

Settlement Paperwork

Settlement paperwork must be memorialized into a Stipulation for Settlement. A Stipulation for Settlement should contain a brief statement of the admitted material facts, a statement of the matters in dispute, the positions of the parties and supporting documentation, and the matters agreed upon by the parties. The Stipulation for Settlement may also include the weekly wage at the time of injury, the compensation rate, prior payments made by the employer/insurer and third parties (intervenors), statements concerning entitlement to wage adjustments and specific statements concerning vocational rehabilitation services and medical expenses, including whether they have been paid and by whom, as well as other information specific to your case. The Stipulation for Settlement will often include a section on attorney fees and costs that will be paid. Finally, the Stipulation for Settlement will state what the employer/insurer is paying you in exchange for the claims for specific workers' compensation benefits you are giving up. The Stipulation for Settlement may also state what the employer/insurer is paying to other third parties (intervenors).

Make sure you understand the type of settlement the employer/insurer is offering and what benefits your settlement will affect. The benefits you are entitled to are controlled by the law on the date you were injured. Ask questions so that you clearly understand what you are giving up and what you are getting in return.

Vacating a Past Stipulation for Settlement

The Workers' Compensation Court of Appeals can set aside a settlement for good cause if it was based on fraud or a mistake of both parties or if there is newly discovered evidence or a substantial change in the employee's medical condition. You should never enter into a final settlement with the expectation that you can reopen it later. The court is reluctant to set aside settlements.

If you are wishing to vacate a prior settlement, speak with an experienced workers' compensation lawyer. Our office is knowledgeable in vacating a Stipulation for Settlement.

CHAPTER 9
FREQUENTLY ASKED QUESTIONS ABOUT THE WORKERS' COMPENSATION LITIGATION PROCESS

THE MINNESOTA WORKERS' litigation process can be lengthy and confusing. Every case is different involving unique facts, claims and defenses. Make sure you understand your rights and options. If you are represented by an attorney, your attorney is the best person to answer your questions.

What happens after an Employee's Claim Petition is filed?

The filing of a Claim Petition begins a formal litigation process. Not every case proceeds in exactly the same way, but generally the steps in the litigation process include: the filing of an Answer to your claim by the Employer/Insurer; a period of discovery often including the deposition of the employee (you) and possibly other witnesses; an examination by a doctor of the employer/insurer's choice; assignment of the file to a compensation judge at the Office of Administrative Hearings (OAH); a settlement conference; a pretrial conference if the case does not settle; and if the case does not settle, a hearing before the compensation judge at which your claims will be decided by the judge.

What is discovery?

Discovery is a process where each party finds out about the basic facts and defenses of the claim. Documents that are useful for settlement or a hearing are gathered including medical records and bills, witness statements, wage information, etc. Information about the claim is compiled and exchanged between the attorneys. Depositions and examinations by expert witnesses are part of the discovery process.

What is a deposition?

A deposition, you give testimony under oath. It is like testimony at a hearing, except there is no judge present. Depositions of the employee and other witnesses are taken to find out what you or other witnesses know and to establish as many facts about the case before a hearing. Your employer or its insurer has the right to depose you. In addition, anyone who has information related to your case can be deposed.

Can the insurer require me to be seen by their doctor?

Yes. You can be required to be examined by a doctor chosen and paid by the employer/insurer. The insurer's doctor will not treat you. The insurer's doctor will provide the employer/insurer with a report answering certain questions asked by the employer/insurer concerning your injury and claims.

What is an intervenor?

An intervenor is a health care provider, insurance company, government agency or anyone else that has something to gain or lose in a hearing about your claim. Typically, an intervenor is seeking to be paid for a benefit it has provided for you, such as medical or chiropractic care.

You should provide your attorney with the details of all medical providers who have treated you for your work injury and any other health insurance you or your spouse have that may have paid for any of the medical treatment you received for your work injury. Also be sure to tell your attorney about any wage-loss or income-replacement benefits you have received from any source (such as unemployment or short-term or long-term disability benefits).

It is important you provide information about potential intervenors to your attorney because the lack of proper notification to any potential intervenors can delay your claim. This is true whether your claim is decided in a hearing before a judge or is resolved through a settlement agreement.

What is a workers' compensation settlement?

When people use the term "settlement," it refers to a written agreement reached by the employee and employer/insurer. It is usually prepared by the attorneys and signed by the employee and insurer. The agreement often requires an employee to give up the right to past and future benefits. In return, the employee receives a specific sum of money from the employer/insurer.

A settlement conference will automatically be scheduled to take place approximately six months after your Claim Petition is filed. The six months allows both sides to complete their discovery, take any depositions they wish to take, secure doctors' reports, and make sure they fully understand the claims, defenses and likely value of the case. If less than six months is required for these steps, you can request a settlement conference be scheduled earlier.

What is a hearing and what can I expect?

A hearing is the formal trial of your claims before a compensation judge. It is similar to a District Court trial but not as formal. There are no juries in workers' compensation trials. Hearings are recorded so that a record can be transcribed in the event of an appeal. You will testify at your hearing. Your attorney will ask you questions to help you explain to the judge how your injury occurred, and all of the basic facts involved in your case.

The attorney for the employer/insurer will also get to ask you questions during "cross exam." Other witnesses may also testify. The attorneys will introduce into evidence various written exhibits including your medical records and bills, and wage loss information. Hearings in workers' compensation cases can usually be completed in half a day, but sometimes take longer. The judge should issue a decision within 60 days of your hearing. You may appeal a judge's decision if you disagree with it. The Workers' Compensation Court of Appeals will decide the appeal.

Should I settle my case or go to hearing?

The decision about whether to settle your case or proceed to a hearing is an important one. You should discuss this thoroughly with your attorney if you are represented. Make sure you understand the type of settlement the insurer is offering and what benefits your settlement will affect. Ask questions so that you clearly understand what you are giving up and what you are getting in return.

For example, if you agree to a full, final and complete settlement with only medical benefits open, the only type of benefit you can claim after the settlement are those medical benefits. You will receive no wage-loss benefits of any kind and no vocational rehabilitation services to assist in your return-to-work efforts. The trade-off is you will generally receive a lump-sum cash payment at the time of settlement.

Can I sue my employer directly other than for workers' compensation benefits?

Direct Cause of Action Against the Employer.

Minnesota law allows an employee to directly sue his or her employer for one year of wages if the employer refuses to offer the employee continued employment if employment is available within the employee's physical restrictions. The employer must have at least 50 employees to be subject to this cause of action. Further, the maximum amount an employee can sue for is $15,000. This action must be brought in District Court.

Although the Workers' Compensation Act does allow a direct cause of action for gross negligence with a knowing waiver of workers' compensation benefits, there has never been a successful case brought in Minnesota as of the date of this update. This was shown in the Cory Stringer case whose estate tried to sue the Vikings directly but lost. You may still have a direct cause of action against a negligent third party who is not your employer.

Employer cannot obstruct Employee seeking workers' compensation benefits.

It is unlawful for an employer to discharge (or fire) an employee for seeking workers' compensation benefits. It is also unlawful for an employer to even threaten to discharge an employee or reduce an employee's pay or benefits for seeking workers' compensation benefits.

Minnesota Statute §176.82, subd. 1 provides that:

> *"Any person discharging or threatening to discharge an employee for seeking workers' compensation benefits . . . is liable in a civil action for damages incurred by the employee including . . . costs and reasonable attorney fees, and for punitive damages not to exceed three times the amount of any compensation benefit to which the employee is entitled."*

There is a three part test to determine if an employer is liable under Minn. Stat. §176.82.

1. That the employee engaged in "protected conduct" (sought workers' compensation benefits); and

2. That an "adverse employment action" was taken by the employer (fired or threatened to fire the employee or reduce the employee's pay or benefits); and

3. That there was a causal connection between the protected conduct and the adverse employment action.

If an employer violates Minn. Stat. § 176.82, an employee may recover compensatory damages. The court may also order the employer to pay damages for mental anguish and suffering, in addition to punitive damages in an amount not more than three times the compensatory damages. An employee who successfully recovers under these claims is entitled to recover attorneys' fees and litigation costs.

If you feel that your employer is treating you differently because of a workers' compensation injury, please call us to discuss. It costs you nothing to talk with us.

CHAPTER 10
GLOSSARY OF TERMS

Accepted Claim – A claim that the insurer agrees to pay for the injury or illness. This does not mean however that this will always be the case. An insurer can later deny benefits even if they have paid benefits in the past

ADA – Americans with Disabilities Act – A federal law that prohibits discrimination against employees with disabilities.

Adjudicate -To act as a judge; to settle.

Admin Conf – Administrative Conference.

Administrative law – Body of law that governs the running of administrative agencies. The rules and regulations created by administrative agencies.

Admissible evidence – Evidence which may be introduced in court and considered by the judge.

Adjuster – See Claims Representative.

Affidavit – A written statement sworn to or affirmed before a person with authority to witness the oath.

Affirmative defense – A defendants' answer to a claim petition which is more than a denial of the Employees charges and which presents evidence or arguments in favor of the defendant.

Aggravation – A circumstance which increases the seriousness or adds to the injury.

ALJ – See Compensation Judge.

Answer – The first response or pleading made by the defendant/Insurer to the claims made in the Claim Petition.

Appellant – The one appealing the decision or order.

Award – See Stipulation.

AWW – Average Weekly Wage – The wage used to calculate workers' compensation benefits.

Burden of proof – Obligation to provide evidence necessary to establish a disputed fact or degree of belief in the mind of the court. In Worker's Compensation matters typically it is the employee who bears the burden of proof. The Employee needs to establish by a preponderance of the evidence that the work injury is a substantial contributing cause to the disputed benefits.

Case Manager – Not to be confused with a Claims Representative or even a QRC. They are not the same. A Case Manager will typically be assigned to the file by the insurance company or insurer to look over the case and to keep an eye on the employee. This is often a nurse that gets involved with you and your treating physician. They do not have to abide by the same rules and regulations of a QRC. They are agents of the insurance company and may not have the best interests of the injured worker in mind.

Causation – The necessary link between an injury and the resulting damages or condition.

Clmt – Claimant, employee, injured worker, petitioner, etc.

Claims Representative – Is the person who handles your claim on behalf of the insurance company.

Closed – A term used when certain benefits are no longer available to the employee based on a prior agreement or decision. This should not be confused with a file that has been "administratively" closed. Oftentimes, insurance companies will claim that the file is "closed" although the injured workers are still entitled to benefits under the law.

CT - Cumulative injury. See also Gillette Injury. May also refer to a CT scan which is a diagnostic tool used to evaluate an injury.

Compensation Judge – CJ – This is the judge that may hear your case. Unlike civil court, in Minnesota, there is no jury and cases are heard before a compensation judge.

Contingent fee – A fee paid to a lawyer depending on the amount awarded in the litigation. This may be nothing if the suit is lost.

COD – Certificate of Dispute – A form used to let the State know that a dispute has arisen regarding entitlement to certain benefits.

Claim Petition – CP – A form filed with the State to request payment of various benefits.

CMCP – Certified Managed Care Plans -An employee covered by managed care selects a treating doctor from the network, which must include medical doctors, chiropractors, osteopaths, podiatrists, physical and occupational therapists, and specialists. An employee is not required to receive treatment for a work injury from a specific network of providers if notice of coverage has not been given or if the managed care plan is not certified.

Death Benefits – If an employee dies as a result of a work-related injury, the dependents under the law may be entitled to dependency benefits.

DA – Defense Attorney. This is the attorney that represents the insurance company

DDD – Degenerative disc disease.

DEED – Minnesota Department of Employment and Economic Development.

Def – Defendant. See DA.

Dependency Benefits – See Death Benefits.

Deposition–A deposition is sworn testimony in front of a court reporter.

Denied Claim – When the insurance company denies payment of benefits to the injured worker. This is typically done by a letter, an Answer or in a Notice of Insurers' Primary Liability Determination.

Disability Rating – See permanent partial disability rating or PPD.

Dispute – A disagreement about your right to payments, services or benefits.

D & O – Decision and Order.

DOI – Date of injury.

DOL – Date of Loss.

DOLI – Minnesota Department of Labor and Industry

EE – Employee.

ER – Employer.

FCE – Functional Capacities Evaluation.

FD – Full Duty.

FFC – Full, Final and Complete Settlement.

FMLA – Family and Medical Leave Act.

F & O – Findings and Order – A written decision by a workers' compensation judge regarding your case. The F & O becomes final if not appealed to the WCCA within 30 days.

Filing – Sending or delivering a document to a government agency as part of the legal process. Filing means the date the document is received by the agency.

F & O – Finding and Order.

FROI – First Report of Injury.

Future Medical – The right to claim future medical treatment for a work injury

GP – General Physician

Gillette Injury – An injury caused by repeated events or repeated exposures to work.

Heaton – A type of attorney fees.

Hearing – A legal proceeding where a judge will consider evidence, testimony and arguments concerning the case in order to make a decision concerning a dispute.

HIPPA – HIPAA is an acronym that stands for a federal law, enacted in 1996, the Health Insurance Portability and Accountability Act (HIPAA).

IR – Insurer.

INT– Intervenor – A party that joins the workers' compensation claim to assert a right to payment or reimbursement. Typically, these will be medical providers, third party payors, government entities, etc.

IME– Independent Medical Examination or Adverse Medical Examination (AME).

Impairment Rating – See permanent partial disability or PPD.

IR – Insurer.

Judge – See Compensation Judge.

LD – Light Duty.

Mediation – A voluntary conference with an independent party who acts as a mediator whose person is to help facilitate a settlement amongst the parties.

Medical Treatment – Treatment that is reasonable and necessary to cure and relieve the effects of a work-related injury.

Modified work – When accommodations have been made to your work duties based on your physical condition.

Notice– When the employer has been advised of a work-related injury. There are deadlines for reporting a work-related injury.

OAH –Office of Administrative Hearings

OSHA –Occupational Safety and Health Act

Permanent Partial Disability -A monetary payment for loss of impairment or function.

PPD – Permanent Partial Disability Benefits.

PTD – Permanent Total Disability Benefits.

Penalty –An amount of money you get when things were not done correctly by the employer or insurer. The type(s) and amount of the penalty depends on the infraction.

QRC – Qualified Rehabilitation Consultant.

Roraff – A type of attorney fees.

RTW – Return to work.

ROM – Range of Motion.

Settlement – An agreement between you and the insurance company regarding your workers' compensation case.

Settlement Conference – SC – A conference scheduled by the court to discuss settlement before trial.

Specific Injury – An injury caused by one event or incident at work.

SSDI – Social Security Disability Benefits- These are long term assistance for totally disabled individuals. These benefits come from the Social Security Administration. They may be reduced by the workers' compensation benefits you receive.

Stipulation – Stip -A settlement agreement amongst the parties where they agree to certain terms. This needs to be approved by an Award which gets signed by a compensation judge. Once an Award has been issued the insurance company has 14 days to make payment.

Subd. 7 fees/Partial Reimbursement of attorney fees – Fees paid to the employee which are calculated based on the employee's attorney's fees.

TTD – Temporary Total Disability Benefits.

TPD – Temporary Partial Disability Benefits

Vocational Rehabilitation – A worker's compensation benefit. This may include the assistance of a QRC, job placement and retraining. The QRC works with the parties to develop a mutually agreeable vocational rehabilitation plan.

Wage loss – The monetary loss an injured worker has from missing work due to their injury. This is paid through workers compensation benefits in the form of TTD, TPD or PTD.

WCCA – Workers Compensation Court of Appeals.

WCAC – Workers Compensation Advisory Council.

WID – Worker identification number – the WID number is person-specific: a unique two- to eight-character number is automatically generated by the State. The WID number may be used rather than the Social Security number, along with the date of injury, to identify a specific case file.

CHAPTER 11
CONCLUSION

THIS BOOK CAN only give you a general overview of the workers' compensation system and the benefits it affords. Each case, including yours, will have its own facts and nuances. Therefore, use this book as a tool to stay educated and empowered, but do not be afraid to ask for help. That is where our office comes in.

I have found that once people talk with me or others at my law firm about their claims and about the legal process, they feel much better and more at ease with the process. After talking with us, they understand what is fair, and they feel good about doing the right thing.

Plus, there is no charge and no pressure to talk with an attorney.

One of the reasons I wrote this book is to see if my firm can help you. We would like to talk with you about your legal rights, and to answer your questions without any pressure.

I would like to offer you a free consultation – You can meet with us at our office, over the phone, or a video conference and we will discuss your legal rights.

It is our hope that during this discussion we can help you with the following:

- Find a way for you to obtain the medical help you need, and to get compensation for your injuries.

- Find out if the insurance company or employer you are up against is withholding benefits you are entitled to or is pressuring you to make a quick settlement.

- See if you might be exposed to risks you may not even know exist, and that could spell disaster for you.

- And to answer all your questions.

We are here to help you!

Our goal is to create a situation where you feel comfortable talking with an expert about your legal options, and to answer any questions you may have. We understand that this can be a very difficult time.

After reviewing this book, you probably have thought of a few more questions. Feel free to call us while this is still fresh in your mind. Waiting any longer may just cause more stress or put you at greater risk. We would be happy to get you the information that could ease your mind.

You may be wondering how we earn our money, and whether you will have to pay an hourly fee. Please understand that we only get compensated when we collect disputed money for our clients. We only get paid if you get paid.

We believe we have a duty as lawyers to educate members of the public about their rights and responsibilities. We try to do this through our web sites and our newsletters. We hope you will look at all we do. We also hope that you find our work to be helpful to you.

CHAPTER 12
FORMS

Work Injury Information

Date of Injury(ies) _____

Did I Report the Injury: Yes/No

Reported to who: _____

Employer _____

AWW$ _____

Address of Employer: _____

Work Comp Insurer _____

Claims Rep: _____

Phone No. _____

Address _____

City/St/Zip _____

Claim No. _____

QRC: _____

Addreess _____

Phone No. _____

Important Phone Numbers

Mottaz & Sisk (855)354-2667 or (763) 421-8226

Dept of Labor and Industry - (651)284-5030

QRC: _____

Claims Rep: _____

Doctors:
1. _____
2. _____
3. _____
4. _____
5. _____
6. _____

<u>Appointments</u>
1. _____
2. _____
3. _____

Mileage and Parking Form

MILEAGE/PARKING EXPENSES

Name: _____ WID#: _____
W.C. Insurer: _____
Claim No.: _____ DOI: _____

Date	Medical Provider	RT Miles	Parking Expense

Job Logs

JOB SEARCH RECORD

CLIENT NAME: _____

WEEK OF: _____
(Monday's Date)

DATE	COMPANY (Name/Address)	EMPLOYER REP (Name/Title)	TYPE CONTACT (Pers. or Phone)	OUTCOME	FOLLOW-UP PLAN

Form Created by Jerry Sisk (763)421-8226

Made in the USA
Middletown, DE
19 October 2024